The Wolf Song in Me

AAhhhOOooo

Written by
Marnie O. Mamminga

Illustrated by
Mary C. Parks

This book or any portion thereof may not be reproduced or used in any manner whatsoever without the express written permission of the publisher, except for the use of brief quotations in a book review.

Contact Marnie O. Mamminga and Mary C. Parks at marniemamminga.com

Publisher's Cataloging-in-Publication Data
Names: Mamminga, Marnie O., author. | Parks, Mary C., 1950- illustrator.
Title: The wolf song in me / Marnie O. Mamminga ; Mary C. Parks, illustrator.
Description: Batavia, IL : Deerpath Road Press, 2024. | Series: Finding wisdom in nature, bk. 2. | Includes bibliographical references and index. | Summary: A child sees wolf tracks on a forest road, teaching the creative power of observing nature. | Audience: Grades K-4.
Identifiers: ISBN 978-0-9800529-8-5 (paperback) | ISBN 978-0-9881993-3-0 (hardcover)
Subjects: LCSH: Picture books for children. | High interest-low vocabulary books. | CYAC: Wolves--Fiction. | Nature--Fiction. | Animal tracks--Fiction. | BISAC: JUVENILE FICTION / Animals / Wolves, Coyotes & Wild Dogs. | JUVENILE FICTION / Concepts / Sounds. | JUVENILE FICTION / Science & Nature / Trees & Forests. | JUVENILE FICTION / Readers / Beginner.
Classification: LCC PZ7.1.M26 Wo 2024 (print) | DDC [E]--dc23.

LCCN: 2024920670

Copyright 2024, Marnie O. Mamminga and Mary C. Parks
All Rights Reserved

Deerpath Road Press
Batavia, IL

In memory of my father, who encouraged my brothers and sisters and me as children to listen for and to love the howl of "Willie the Wolf" coming from the north shore wetlands of our cabin's lake: "Don't be afraid. He is calling to his friends."

To my husband, Dave, who over the years has patiently listened with me on many a starlight night for the wolves to sing their magic once again.

And for my grandchildren Alice, Amber, Elena, Emmett, Joy, Lily, Marlo, and Ryan: May you too learn to know and love the mystery of the wolf's song.

~ Marnie O. Mamminga

I dedicate my illustrations to writers who paint pictures with their words, every child that has conveyed to me their sense of discovery and wonder, and most directly, my grandsons, Anthony and Leo, and my son, Brad.

~ Mary C. Parks

Though maybe I should be, for I am walking with wolves.

Usually, there is only one set of wolf tracks, but on this golden morning, smaller wolf tracks have joined a bigger leader.

The tracks parallel each other, like buddies on a walk.

As I follow along, it's as though I have joined them in a bond of friendship.

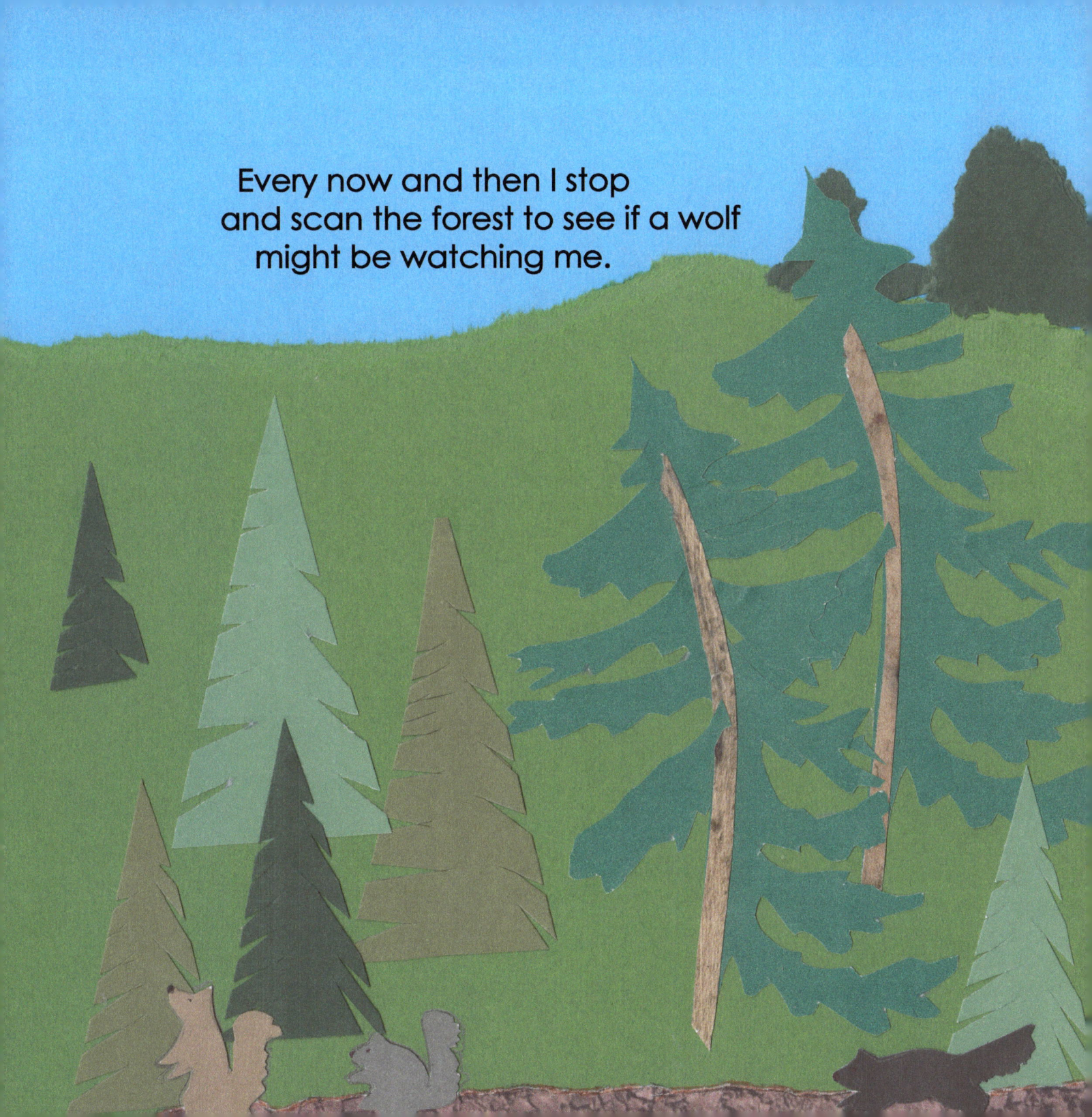

Home

In fact, I find it comforting to know such wild, intelligent creatures are willing to share their beautiful woodland home with me.

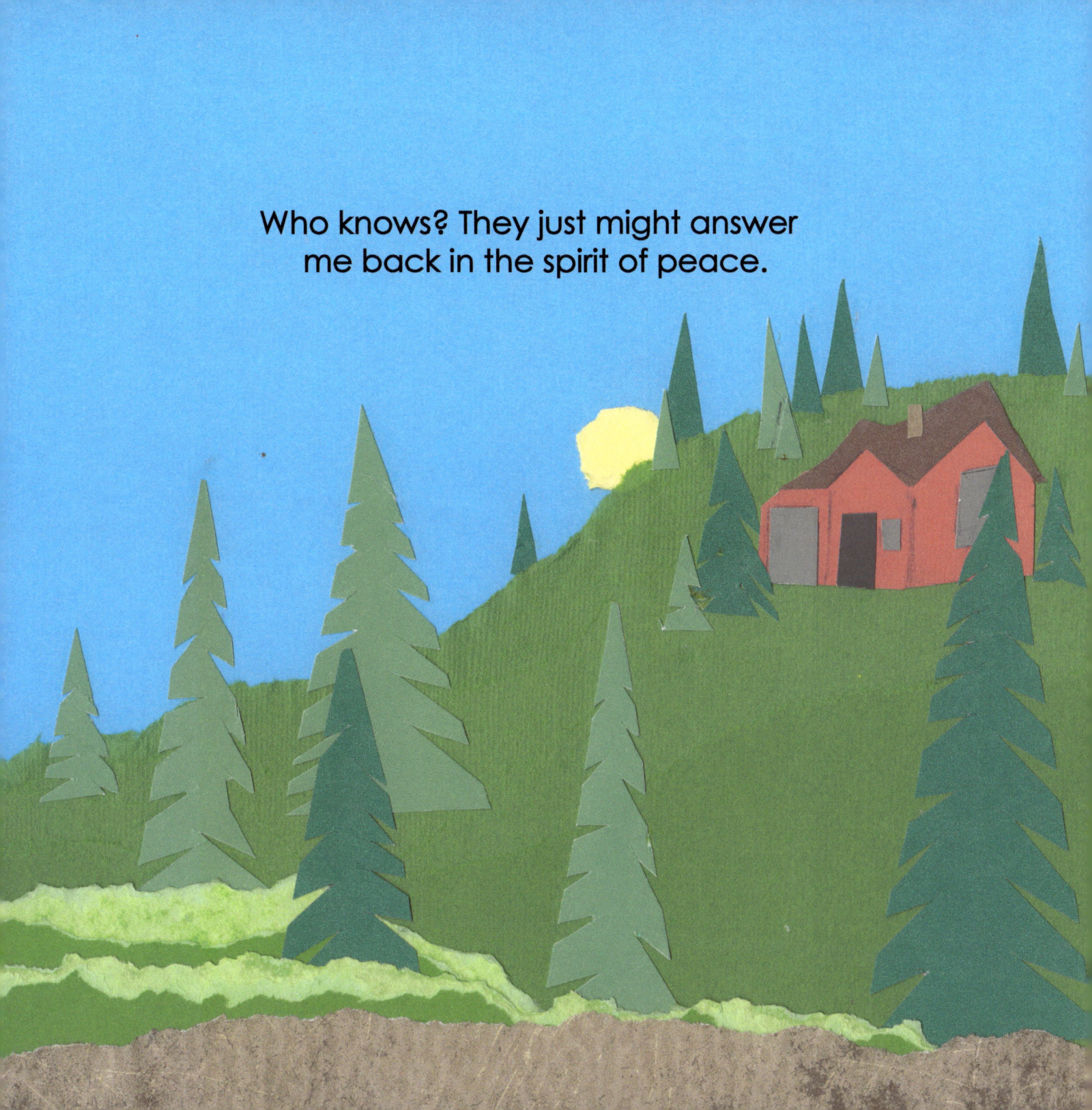

AAhhhOOooO

PEACE

Wolf Fun Facts

1. Wolves typically avoid people.
2. They howl to communicate with each other.
3. A wolf's fur can be brownish gray but also white or black.
4. The wolf's average foot size is 4" wide x 5" long.
5. Wolves can run up to 38 mph.
6. Common food for wolves is elk, deer, and moose.
7. Wolf pups weigh only one pound at birth, but around three weeks they are ready to leave their den and explore their world.

Source: International Wolf Center, Ely, Minnesota.
Would you like to see a real wolf?
We invite you to go to the International Wolf Center website:
https://wolf.org

DISCUSSION QUESTIONS

1. Do you sometimes feel afraid? If so, what frightens you?

2. How do you calm your fears?

3. When you are out in nature, what do you like to discover?

4. How many animals, birds, and tree colors can you find?

5. What colors and clothing show you it is early autumn?

6. How do the pictures help "tell" the story?

Follow the magic circles...

...to draw your own wolf.

Meet the Author

Marnie O. Mamminga is the award-winning author of *Return to Wake Robin: One Cabin in the Heyday of Northwoods Resorts* and *On a Clear Night: Essays from the Heartland*. As a former educator, Marnie has also been a professional essayist and features writer for more than 30 years. Her work has been featured on NPR and in numerous regional and national publications, including the *Chicago Tribune*, *Reader's Digest*, *The Christian Science Monitor*, the *Midwest Prairie Review*, *Lake Superior Magazine*, *Detroit Free Press Magazine*, and in several *Chicken Soup for the Soul* books. In addition, she is a frequent perspective contributor for NPR's WNIJ.

∼

The Woodpecker's Song, Mamminga and Parks' first children's book in their *Finding Wisdom in Nature* series, won two prestigious Eric Hoffer awards: Grand Prize Short List and First Runner Up in the children's category. Find out more about Marnie at her website: marniemamminga.com.

Meet the Illustrator

Mary C. Parks was born and raised in the suburban Midwest. These illustrations are intuitive to exploring the awe of autumn days with her curious son, Brad, and young grandsons, Anthony and Leo. As a national and state acclaimed art teacher of thirty-five years, kindergarten through the college level, Mary also published her works in ILLUSTRATOR magazine for four years and illustrated several cookbooks. Retirement unfolded an unanticipated life for this multi-technique artist. While art history, travel, technology, and trends contribute, Mary's art echoes the spirit of her heartland roots.

∼

"Art is the voice that uses no words; it sees, listens, and reflects. My illustrations for *The Wolf Song in Me* were inspired by nature's glory and by reflecting on the enlightening words of author Marnie O. Mamminga. It is my hope that our words and illustrations awaken the imaginative wonder in the minds of children."

M.C.P.

Acknowledgments

Again, my heartfelt thanks: To Sue Stephens and Dan Klefstad for encouraging me to write WNIJ perspectives for NPR from which this story sprang; to my sisters, Mary and Nancy, for their keen insight and support; Sammi and Gary King for always lending a helping hand or a listening ear; to all the dear friends who have enthusiastically spread the word about our books; and to Christine Keleny of CKBooks Publishing for her patience, guidance, and expertise in making our dreams come true.

Most especially to Mary C. Parks, illustrator extraordinaire, who not only brings amazing art to the page but does so with an intuitive wisdom and creative vision that continually surprises and delights.

To my sons, John, Bob, and Tom, and daughters-in-law, Lara and Jennifer, whose support and encouragement are always at the ready.

And, as always, to my husband, Dave, for all his behind-the-scenes efforts that continually ease the way on my writing journey.

~ Marnie O. Mamminga

When a writer possesses the talent to express words filled with visual imagery, an illustrator's assignment is immediately sparked with readiness to create.

Thank you, Marnie, for inviting children and me outdoors to see, explore, and discover animals' distinctive foot tracks and, per chance, to hear their songs in the autumn woodlands.

Thank you for a second time to publisher Christine Keleny for her knowledge, technical assistance, insightful ideas, and guidance.

To all our kind supporters, thank you for your many presentation invitations, shout-outs, and promotions that helped launch our first book, *The Woodpecker's Song*, and inspire our second, *The Wolf Song in Me*.

A special appreciation to my grandsons, Anthony and Leo Parks, for taking the time to tear all the tiny colored leaves to apply to suitable pages.

"Explore, Dream, Discover" – Mark Twain

~ Mary C. Parks

Next up......*Songs of the Lake*

The Wolf Song in Me follows **The Woodpecker's Song** in the Finding Wisdom in Nature Series. Both books seek to encourage children to find the peace, beauty, and surprise that the natural world offers. Completing the Songs in Nature Trilogy, **Songs of the Lake** is already in progress.

Stay tuned…

www.ingramcontent.com/pod-product-compliance
Lightning Source LLC
Chambersburg PA
CBHW042143290426
44110CB00002B/101